AMAZING ANIMALS

FROM AROUND THE WORLD

ILLUSTRATED BY
PETER DAVID SCOTT

For Pauline—P.D.S.

PIPPBROOK BOOKS

This edition produced in 2010 for Borders Group Inc.

Devised and produced by The Templar Company Limited,
The Granary, North Street, Dorking, Surrey, RH4 1DN, UK
www.templarco.co.uk

Designed by Leonard Le Rolland
Written by Rachel Williams
Edited by Libby Hamilton and Hannah Wilson
Peter David Scott is represented by the Art Agency
www.peterdavidscott.com

Printed in China

AMAZING ANIMALS

FROM AROUND THE WORLD

ILLUSTRATED BY

PETER DAVID SCOTT

PIPPBROOK
BOOKS

THE WESTERN GORILLA
uses calls, facial expressions, and body language to communicate.

THE BIRDS OF PARADISE

are some of nature's greatest show-offs.

THE GOLDEN POISON DART FROG

is one of the most poisonous animals on the planet.

THE SEA HORSE

reverses the roles of parents—
the male carries the young.

THE LIONFISH
is one of the ocean's
most poisonous fish.

THE DUCK-BILLED PLATYPUS

is one of the world's few
egg-laying mammals.

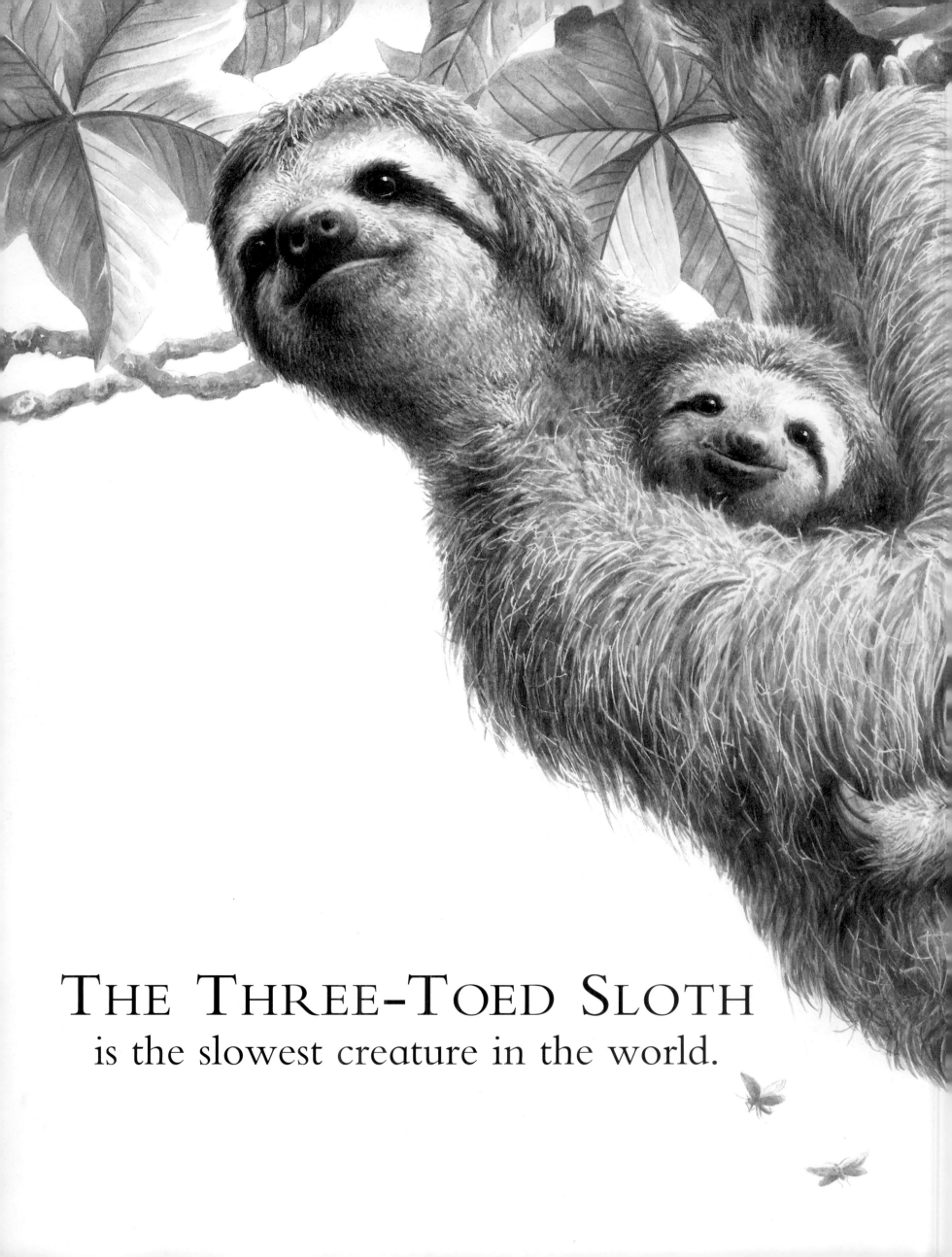

THE THREE-TOED SLOTH
is the slowest creature in the world.

THE EMPEROR PENGUIN
raises its young in the coldest
place on earth.

THE RETICULATED PYTHON
is the world's longest snake.

THE PANTHER
CHAMELEON
shows its feelings through
its skin color.

THE GIANT PANDA
has to spend almost every
waking minute eating.

THE BEAVER
is one of nature's
greatest builders.

THE GIANT TORTOISE

is one of the oldest creatures on earth.

THE CHEETAH
is the fastest animal on land.

THE FRUIT BAT'S
colonies are among the largest
of the animal kingdom.

THE HUMPBACK WHALE
has one of the furthest migrations
of any mammal.

THE OSTRICH
is both the largest of all birds
and the fastest runner.

THE FLYING FISH
uses its tail and fins to
take to the air.

THE ORANGUTAN

is the largest mammal to
spend its life in the trees.

THE
HIPPOPOTAMUS
lets fish swim all over its
body to keep it clean.

THE
COELACANTH
shared the earth with
the dinosaurs.

THE
COLOSSAL SQUID
is a giant of the sea.

Amazing Animals

Field Notes

Discover more about each
amazing animal!

Sketches by
Peter David Scott

Western Gorilla

As night falls in the rainforests of Cameroon and Central Africa, a male western gorilla gives a satisfied "belch." This rumbling noise tells his family that he is happy. Western gorillas are masters of communication: making noises, banging their chests, beating the ground, and using body language. Young gorillas will chuckle when happy or cry when upset, and adult males often whine when they are left alone.

Birds of Paradise

There are forty-seven species of birds of paradise. These creatures are some of nature's greatest show-offs and males will do anything to get noticed by females, from fanning their brightly colored feathers to dancing from side-to-side. If the male manages to impress a female, she will choose him as her mate.

Emperor Bird of Paradise

Ribbon-Tailed Astrapia

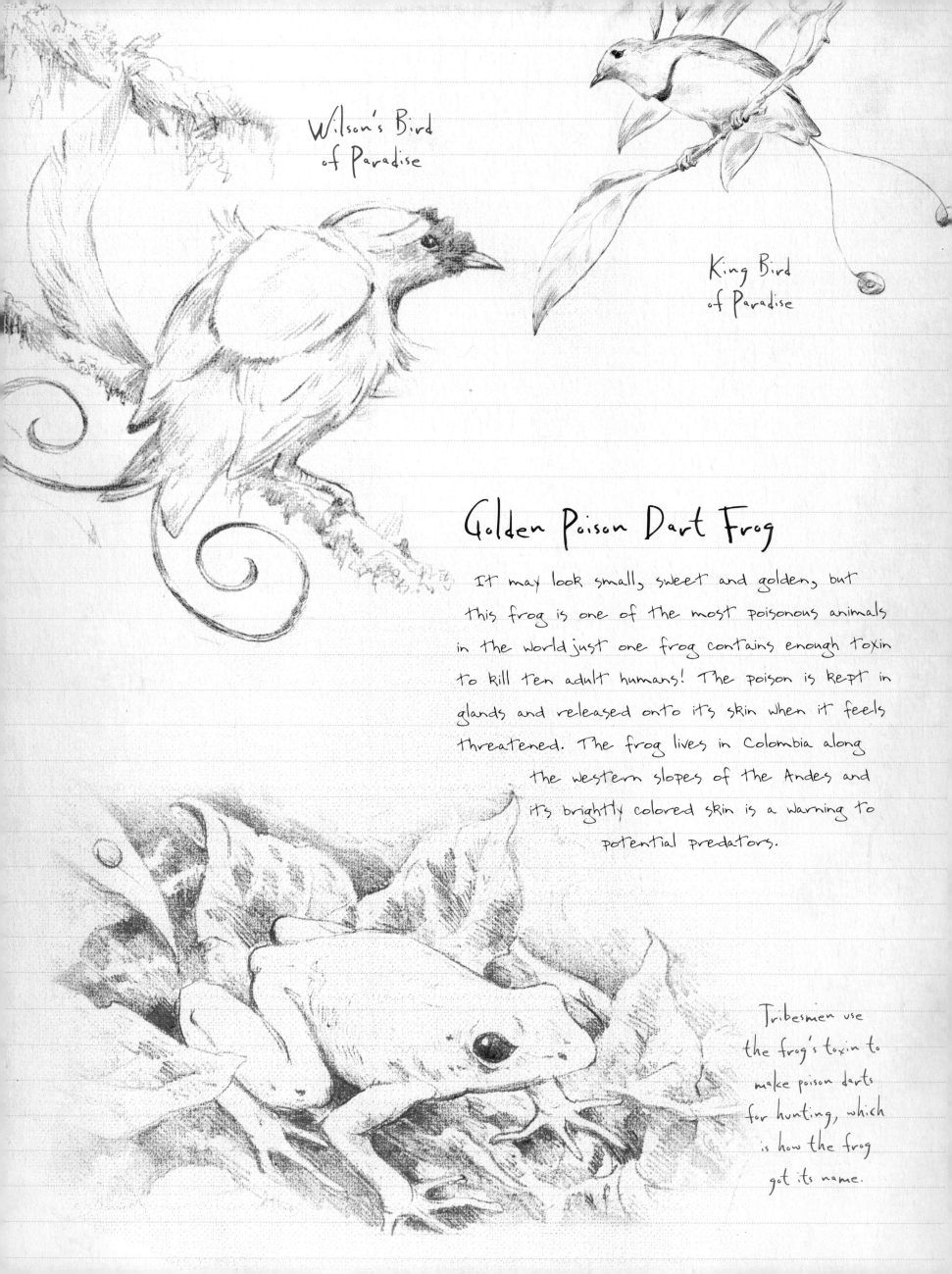

Wilson's Bird
of Paradise

King Bird
of Paradise

Golden Poison Dart Frog

It may look small, sweet and golden, but this frog is one of the most poisonous animals in the world just one frog contains enough toxin to kill ten adult humans! The poison is kept in glands and released onto its skin when it feels threatened. The frog lives in Colombia along the western slopes of the Andes and its brightly colored skin is a warning to potential predators.

Tribesmen use the frog's toxin to make poison darts for hunting, which is how the frog got its name.

Sea Horse

These strange-looking fish are found in shallow tropical waters. Unusually, it is the male and not the female who incubates the eggs. The male sea horse has a big pouch on his front. The female lays her eggs into this pouch, then the male fertilizes the eggs and carries them in it. When they hatch, he releases the baby sea horses into the water.

Lionfish

The lionfish, native to the Indo-Pacific ocean, has one of the most poisonous venoms in the sea and doesn't try to hide it. With its red-and-white zebra stripes and long, showy pectoral fins, everything about the lionfish tells other creatures to stay away. Although it is a fierce predator, this creature only uses its venomous spines for defense. While the venom will not kill a human, it can be deadly for small or medium-sized creatures in seconds.

Duck-Billed Platypus

Living in eastern Australia, the
platypus is one of only two types of mammal
that lay eggs when giving birth. About one month
into her pregnancy, the female will go inside the
burrow she has created out of reeds, then block
the tunnel with earth, and lay her eggs. The
mother platypus will nurse her young until they are
about four months old and can swim on their own.

The duck-billed platypus catches its
prey through electroreception—it can
sense the electric charge given off
when a creature moves its muscles.

Its webbed feet
and long, flat bill
give the platypus
its duck-like
appearance.

The male platypus has
venomous ankle spurs,
which it uses in battle
with other males.

Three-Toed Sloth

This creature moves so little
that moss and algae have time to
grow on it's fur! That is what gives
the sloth a greenish tint, useful camouflage
in the Central and South-American rainforest.
The sloth also has the advantage of three long,
sharp claws, so it can hang for lengthy periods,
and an extra vertebra in it's neck, which allows it to
turn its head in almost a full circle.

All kinds of insect live in the
sloth's fur. There can be up to
a thousand beetles on one sloth.

Emperor Penguin

Emperor penguins are experts
at staying warm in the coldest place
on earth—Antarctica. Huddling together in packs
of up to six thousand, the penguins take turns to
move into the center of the group to shelter from the
icy wind. Females lay their eggs in this harsh environment.
Each female leaves her egg in the care of the male. The male
keeps the egg balanced on his feet, under a feathery pouch of
skin. If an egg touches the ice, it will freeze in seconds.

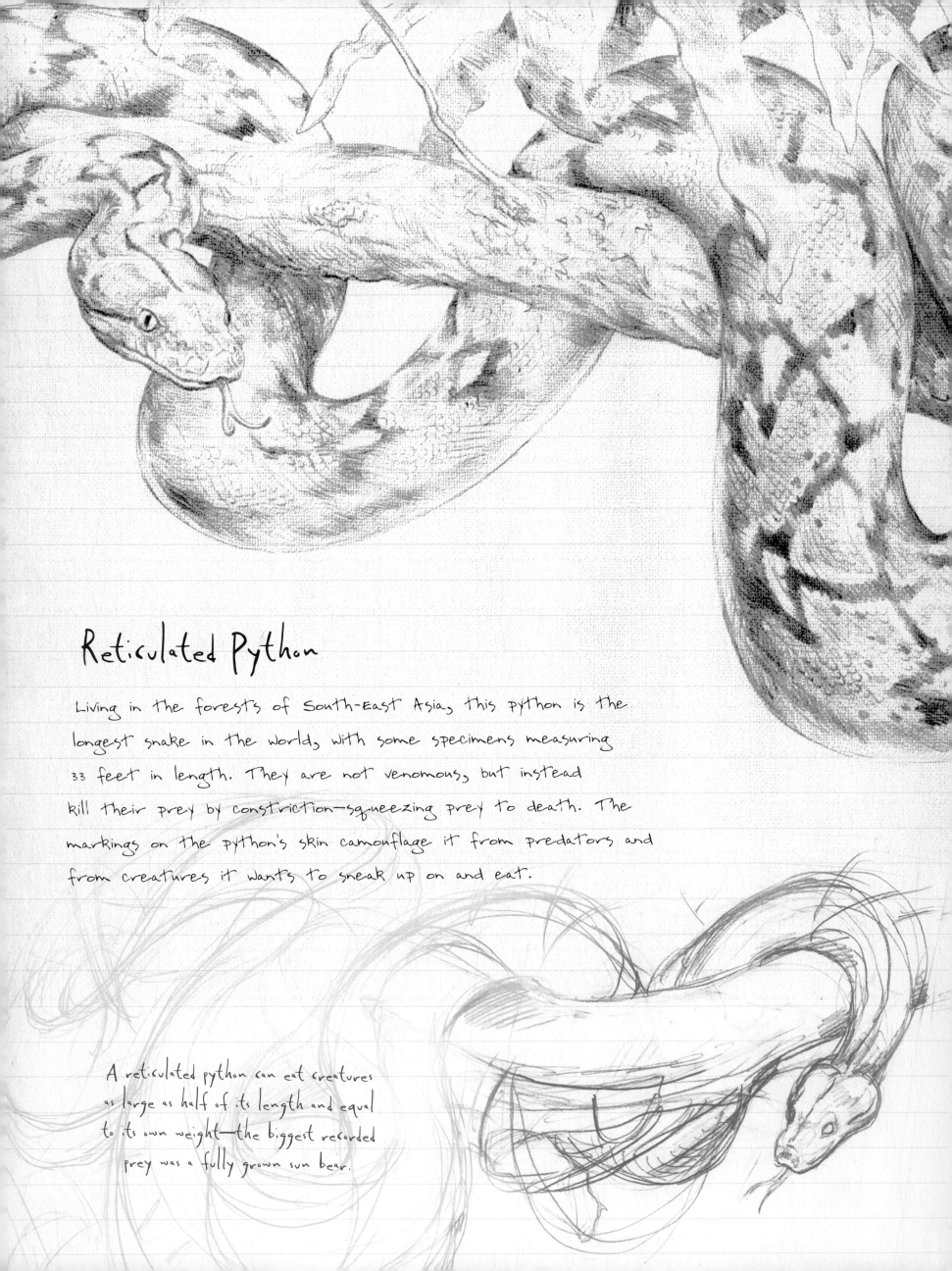

Reticulated Python

Living in the forests of South-East Asia, this python is the longest snake in the world, with some specimens measuring 33 feet in length. They are not venomous, but instead kill their prey by constriction—squeezing prey to death. The markings on the python's skin camouflage it from predators and from creatures it wants to sneak up on and eat.

A reticulated python can eat creatures as large as half of its length and equal to its own weight—the biggest recorded prey was a fully grown sun bear.

Panther Chameleon

In the forests of Madagascar, one animal simply cannot hide its feelings—the panther chameleon. This amazing creature has the ability to change color according to its mood or the temperature due to a substance called melanin that rises towards the surface of its skin. Humans have melanin in their bodies too—it affects hair, eye and skin color. When a panther chameleon's skin turns bright yellow and red, it is angry; when it darkens, it is cold, and when it turns pale, the chameleon is too hot.

Giant Panda

Giant pandas love to eat! These black-and-white bears munch on bamboo for up to 14 hours a day because they need to eat enormous quantities of this leafy grass to stay healthy. Giant pandas are born white—they develop their distinctive black spots as they grow.

North American Beaver

Not many creatures are busier than the beaver! This large, furry rodent is expert at making almost any aquatic environment habitable. Beavers are some of the world's best builders, making huge dams using nearby trees. These massive structures are created to block streams and make ponds, protecting the beaver's home, called a lodge. To keep predators out, the lodge entrance is usually underwater and the beaver covers the outside with fresh mud. This mud dries to become almost as hard as stone, so that no large creatures can force their way inside.

The beaver's flat, paddle-shaped tail and webbed feet make it a great swimmer.

Giant Tortoise

It may be slow, but the giant tortoise of the Galápagos Islands always wins one race—it has one of the longest life spans of any creature on the planet. Most members of this family will live up to a hundred years, and the oldest on record reached 175! During this time it can grow to weigh 661 pounds and be 4 feet in length.

Cheetah

This big cat takes its name from the Hindu word for "spotted one." The cheetah is the fastest creature in the world. Its long legs and slim build make it the perfect sprinter, reaching speeds of up to 62 miles per hour to catch its prey. Running so fast makes the cheetah dangerously hot. They can only sprint for short bursts and must rest straight away afterwards.

Male cheetahs hunt in groups, while females hunt alone.

Fruit Bat

Some creatures are solitary while others,
such as the straw-colored fruit bat, live in
huge colonies that can contain several million
bats. Roosting in tall trees across Africa,
these bats separate into smaller groups to
forage when the sun goes down, searching
out tasty fruit for the colony to share. As
they noisily suck the juice from fruit, these
yellow-chested bats discard the pulp,
scattering seeds across the forest that will
grow into new plants.

Humpback Whale

The humpback whale is one of the world's greatest travelers. Weighing up to 39 tons, these mammals can travel 15,535 miles each year in intimate family pods.
In the summer, they feed in the polar waters. When winter comes, they make the long journey to warmer waters to breed and give birth. During this migration, humpback whales sing "songs"—a sequence of moans, howls and cries— to communicate with other family members.

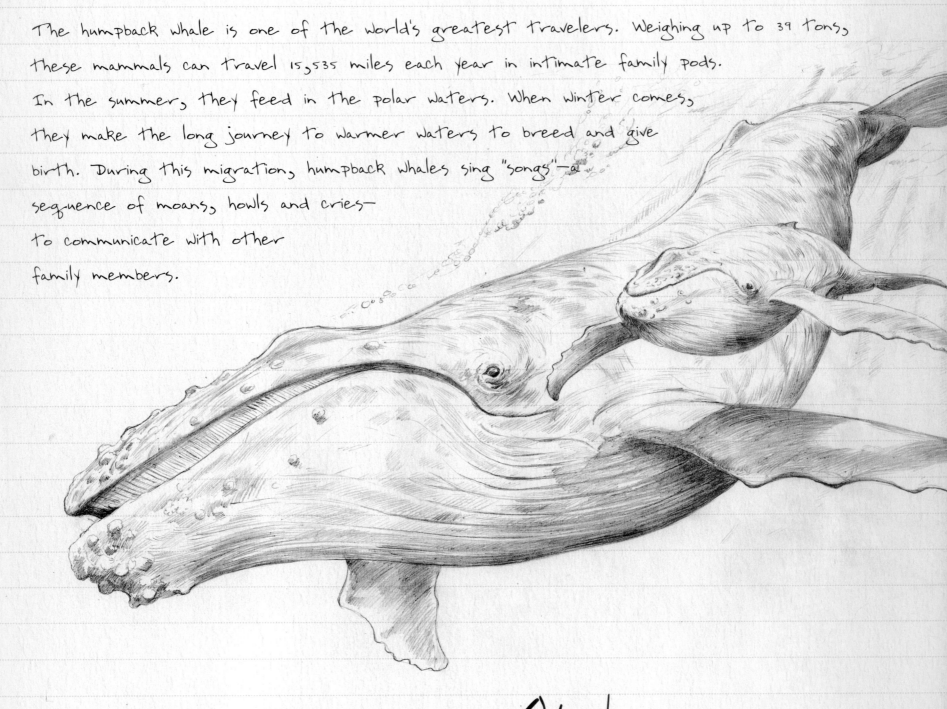

Ostrich

It may not be able to fly, but the native African ostrich can certainly run! This creature is the bird family's fastest runner, reaching speeds of up to 28 miles per hour. The ostrich is also the largest living species of bird, and lays enormous eggs that can weigh up to 4.4 pounds. It is distinctive in its appearance, with a long neck and legs, and billowing, feathered wings.

Orangutan

With an arm span of more than 6.5 feet, the orangutan lives its whole life in the trees of the rainforests of Sumatra and Borneo. These long-haired, orange-colored animals are the largest mammals to eat, sleep, and live in the treetops. Highly intelligent, orangutans have adapted so well to life in the trees that they've even learned to use large leaves as umbrellas when it rains.

The hands of orangutans are very similar to human hands, with four fingers and a thumb.

Flying fish can be found in all the oceans, especially warmer waters.

Flying Fish

Flying fish spend more time out of the water than any other fish. Outnumbered by their enemies—mackerel, tuna and swordfish—flying fish have evolved a remarkable means of escape. Their streamlined torpedo shape helps them gather speed underwater and break the surface without slowing down. Once in the air, their wing-like pectoral fins can keep them airborne for up to 45 seconds.

This cattle egret picks insects
off the skin of the hippopotamus.

African
Barbel Fish

Hippopotamus

Although the hippo can frighten attackers with an open-mouthed roar,
it also lets itself be pampered. During the day, it rests and rolls about
in the rivers and pools of sub-Saharan Africa, accompanied by its very own
personal groomers—birds, like the cattle egret, and fish, such as the
African barbel and the freshwater wrasse. Whole shoals of fish rely on the
hippo for food including its dung and any ticks and parasites living on its
skin. The fish also swim into the hippo's open mouth, picking out food
scraps lodged there and cleaning the hippo's teeth in the process.

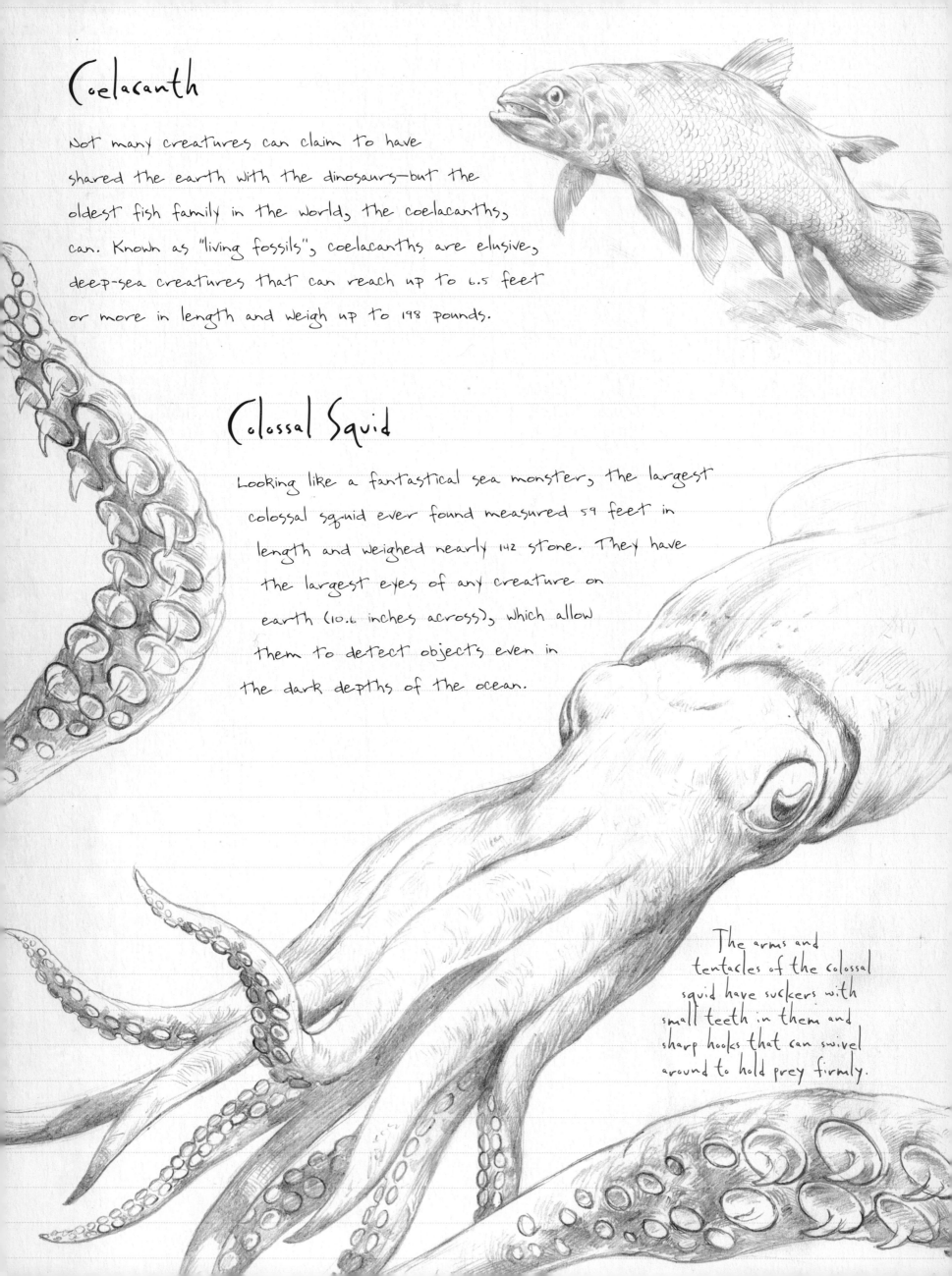

Coelacanth

Not many creatures can claim to have shared the earth with the dinosaurs—but the oldest fish family in the world, the coelacanths, can. Known as "living fossils", coelacanths are elusive, deep-sea creatures that can reach up to 6.5 feet or more in length and weigh up to 198 pounds.

Colossal Squid

Looking like a fantastical sea monster, the largest colossal squid ever found measured 59 feet in length and weighed nearly 142 stone. They have the largest eyes of any creature on earth (10.6 inches across), which allow them to detect objects even in the dark depths of the ocean.

The arms and tentacles of the colossal squid have suckers with small teeth in them and sharp hooks that can swivel around to hold prey firmly.

Peter David Scott